First published 2018 John Vanek

Second edition published 2021 John Vanek

ISBN 978 1 999637 001 9

Price £9.95

You can find out more about John at

www.vaneklifecoach.com

Foreword

'Let Me Do That Too!' is dedicated to all the individuals and groups I have had the privilege of working with over the years.

I thank the clients who have permitted me to coach them with social inclusion techniques, I have witnessed them access activities of their own choice in the mainstream world. Several of them appear with their stories in the book, with only a name change to protect their privacy.

My clients have invariably been people previously excluded from mainstream society as a result of long-term mental health conditions. Even when they had been allowed access, it was often under clinical monitoring and in so-called 'special' settings. No one should be denied open access to the things they want to do.

I also wish to thank the health commissioners who believed in these approaches to mental health and promoted it as part of statutory health programmes. Despite funding being slashed and despite trends in mental health changing, there are strong signs that these methods are being promoted anew.

I am certain that these approaches are solid and valuable. Already we are seeing signs of re-validation and re-dedication to health strategies that are of proven success to individuals' recovery and healing.

The coaching strategies that appear in this book are of great value to anyone who wishes to identify areas where they want to see change in their lives. These have been developed for people previously denied life

coaching. Now I offer them to the whole world, to the privileged and not so privileged alike.
I also wish to thank the mainstream venues and outlets that have welcomed my clients to their creative spaces. They are too numerous to mention but I wish to specifically thank John Merriman, Director of Crown Lane Studio in the London borough of Merton. His creative trainings continue to be invaluable.

Finally, I want to thank anyone who is involved in the arts, whether as a practitioner or provider. The power of the arts to heal, whether through music, visual arts, storytelling or many other forms, cannot be refuted. Countless studies attest to its healing qualities.

A very special thanks goes to my wife Margaret.

Downloads

NB. *There are practical coaching forms and tools in this book. Email me for any downloadable copies of any coaching tools herein.*

vaneklifecoach@gmail.com

Table of Contents

Introduction

Every new step begins with awareness. Awareness that we need to change precedes our knowledge of how to bring it about. The key thing is to be conscious of the need to take that first step.

We don't know what we don't yet know. But in order to begin to know we need to be aware of the fact that we don't yet know.

The purpose of this book is to show how some straightforward life coaching and mentoring techniques have enabled hundreds of people to break through the restrictive precincts of a mental ill-health diagnosis. In turn this has permitted individuals and groups to progress towards independent living based on their own choices, goals, hopes and aspirations.

This book is for anyone with an interest in health and wellbeing. It is for people operating in the health sphere, counsellors, coaches, clinicians, therapists as well as those who provide any kind of service to people in the mainstream community.

This book is for coaches who wish to extend their skills into areas they might not have considered previously. It is a book for health commissioners who want to study the cost-effective and proven strategies that have helped so many people.

Instructional Handbook

'Let me Do That Too' contains tools that can be downloaded for your own coaching practice, consultations and assessments.

These include the social inclusion wheel of life and action plan. It also contains case studies of clients who have used and benefited from, the strategies detailed in this book.

Rationale

Life coaching is designed to help people. Not just some people but all those who want to experience its benefits. It's for people who might have experienced mental ill health as well as for those who haven't.

The same techniques are utilised. The same tools and the same strategies. The important thing is that people who have experienced mental ill health are not excluded from life coaching or mentoring. That is one of the key drivers behind this book.

A movement has been evolving in pubic mental health provision over the last fifty years or so. The movement is shifting away from strictly support-based provision towards services that allow for human growth and development. It is still a work in progress, one that has had plenty of setbacks and impediments on the way.

Individuals need other individuals and no person is an island. Life coaching is there to help people discover and make happen the things inside them that they have always wished to bring into being.

On a personal note I should add that this book has been inside me for a long time. The active involvement of my own mentor and coach has been crucial to making it happen.

On a personal note I should add that this book has been inside me for a long time. The active involvement of my own mentor and coach has been crucial to making it happen. Chapter 1. Revolution is the turning of a wheel, pure and simple

Chapter 1 | Revolution is the turning of a wheel, pure and simple

Detailed information and data on mental disorders is relatively new. Classifications of illnesses have been published since 1840. But it wasn't until 1949 that the World Health Organisation (WHO) printed the sixth revision of the International Statistical Classification of Diseases (ICD), which for the first time included a section on mental disorders.

Over the last sixty years or so what used to be uncharted territory has been mapped out in great detail by a wide range of clinical specialists, practitioners and researchers.

First published in 1952, the DSM (Diagnostic and Statistical Manual of Mental Disorders) currently lists over two hundred and fifty-seven disorders.

The original number in the first edition listed just one hundred and six.

With each new edition, the DSM classifies and adds more disorders, along with complex syndromes that may contain different variants within the one classification.

Its publishers The American Psychiatric Association (APA) describe the Manual as:

- the product of more than 10 years of effort by hundreds of international experts in all aspects of mental health.

APA asserts that the DSM is:

- an authoritative volume that defines and classifies mental disorders in order to improve diagnoses, treatment, and research.

The DSM has become a bible for mental health professionals.

Clinicians, researchers, drug regulation agencies, health insurers, pharmaceutical companies, the legal system, and policy makers use it.

The detailed classification of mental conditions is an heroic undertaking that has enabled breakthroughs in medication, research and treatment.

Chapter 2 | The Limitations of Diagnosis

As much as it has its practical uses, there are limitations to a purely diagnosis - led approach. The main danger lies in the application of a clinical label to the individual, reducing him or her to a set of symptoms. The description might be useful as a pointer to further treatment or a care pathway but it can also grip the individual within the boundaries of a narrow definition, sometimes permanently.

Amongst the cohort of people who have benefited directly from life coaching are my own clients. Many are categorised as having 'severe and enduring' mental health conditions. Using the tools and techniques of social inclusion and 'mainstream' coaching, they have started or re-commenced active lives outside clinical settings. Their inspiring stories appear throughout this book.

Case Study No. 1 | David's Story

David

I first met David one spring. He was referred to me from the Community mental health team and was one of my first clients in my role as a social inclusion bridge builder. I knew very little about him except that he enjoyed playing guitar. This was key information as it meant that David might benefit from the skills of an arts bridge builder like myself to help enable him to access music activities in the mainstream community.

The first meeting with David took place at the unit where he lived with five other people who had also had had spells in mental hospitals. David was happy there.

Our first meeting didn't look promising to begin with. David was clearly uneasy and anxious. He adopted an almost semi-foetal position on the living-room settee.

He was prompted to give answers to my questions by a well-meaning but misguided home manager. Her blunt interjections did nothing to make him more forthcoming about himself nor about any areas he might wish to follow up in mainstream life.

Thinking that not much progress had been made, I eventually made another appointment with David for us to meet together in a week's time at the nearby Costas.

Just as I was getting up to go, David said: 'Do you want to see my new guitar?' 'Yes' I replied, speaking not only in my role as an arts bridge builder but also as a fellow-musician and enthusiast. David ushered me into his room, where I was immediately struck by a dazzling array of music-related gear.

Back in his secure personal world David became animated and talkative. He showed me round his collection of guitars, music effects, and recording equipment, amplifiers, CDs, music and tech magazines. 'Do you want to hear something I recorded?' he asked.

David's playing was impressive - clearly no slouch he had obviously spent hour upon hour meticulously learning guitar and studying his mentors who included Carlos Santana, Steve Vai and David Gilmour.

I knew then that I would have a reasonably smooth ride signposting David to outlets that suited his own mainstream choices and goals. Any difficulties would not arise from David but if anything, from the detailed red tape of sorting out arrangements through the mental health team.

As it turned out David's clinical team was very helpful. I introduced David to the local recording studio where he chose to do a weekly two-hour rehearsal session, bringing his own guitar. This was deemed to be a key part of his care and recovery plan. Social services were initially tough to work with but eventually agreed to fund it through the 'direct payments' or personal budgets system. Five years on, David continues to make great progress. The recording studio remains one of his main lifelines into accessing mainstream life. He has teamed up with fellow musicians on a variety of projects and was a key contributor to the short animation film 'Mister Fox's Night Out', screened at the Wimbledon International 'shorts' festival.

Many other milestones have been achieved. David took a part-time job as an assistant at the recording studio. He continues to collaborate regularly with other musicians, many of them his peers - mental health survivors.

Still from the animation short 'Mister Fox's Night Out'

Chapter 3 | The Limitations of Diagnosis

None of the milestones that have been achieved by people like David could have come about without the philosophy of social inclusion. Great innovatory practices arise out of great ideas combined with a slow process of development. Ideas gain momentum. They are hidden from view sometimes for a long time. But once their time has come there is no stopping them.

The philosophy of social inclusion has impacted on mental health recovery as well as on its methodologies. A way of thinking that has created care plans and interventions that incorporate clients' goals, hopes, dreams and aspirations. Modes of practice that brought about the methods and tools that allow the individual to self-assess and identify personal aspirations.

Every client who has been through mental health services will already have been clinically appraised many times on the basis of his or her diagnoses and history. A different discussion with the client grounded in goals, hopes and personal priorities enables a break away from purely clinical approaches.
It also permits what can turn out to be highly successful transitions back into mainstream life and social inclusion without prejudice.

A New Recovery Pathway

With detailed case studies, methodologies and downloadable tools, 'Let Me Do that Too!' reveals how life coaching techniques have impacted on mental health and the recovery pathway.

The book also shows how thinking and research around social inclusion has had a major positive effect for people with mental health conditions. It explores how people have been able to address their goals, hopes and dreams, often for the first time. It gives accounts of individuals who have been able to take ownership of their lives and turn their dreams into reality.

The book contains coaching tools downloadable on request that are used for mainstream social inclusion, along with a practical handbook of how to implement them into your own coaching or commissioning practice.

Using these techniques clients, including those with long-term prognoses have been able to make successful inroads back into the mainstream arena from which they may have been excluded, sometimes for years.

None of the revolution has occurred without years of persistent hard work and determination. Much of this has arisen from individuals who have had personal experience of ill-health and hospitalisation. Other people have contributed too - policy makers, inclusion champions, commissioners and third sector organisations bold enough to experiment with change.

Case Study No. 2 | Mike's Story

Mike

I knew Mike before he signed up for mainstream inclusion coaching. He had been regularly attending a mental health drop-in centre for several months. In lots of ways, Mike had started his own journey into mainstream before the coaching started.

For Mike the short bus journey to get to the drop-in was a real challenge. It used to trigger his panic attacks so that he would arrive at the drop-in close to hyperventilating. But he was so determined to get there that bit-by-bit he overcame these unpleasant symptoms. He never requested support from staff or carers for his bus journey and it was his own persistence that enabled him to cope and eventually triumph in this small but significant area.

Mike identified one major goal during the life coaching sessions. He told me that he wanted to go back to church and resume a regular pattern of worship. He had lost touch with it for nearly twenty years, since the death of his father.

This was a very simple and clear goal of Mike's. As part of the coaching consultation I asked Mike how much or how little support he required to help achieve this goal. He said that he needed someone to go with him to the church service in the first instance.

As part of my role I was happy to go with Mike to the church one Sunday. Mike was delighted to renew his link with worship and has been attending regularly ever since without any request for extra support.

Chapter 4 | The Impact of Social History

Rosa Parks in 1955 with Martin Luther King

When it comes to mental health, we should not forget the broader sweep of social history. The impact of the civil rights movement going back to the 1950s and further has been significant. On December 1, 1955, in Montgomery, Alabama, Parks refused to obey a bus driver's order to give up her seat in the "colored section" to a white passenger.

Rosa Parks' act of resistance back in 1955 is as significant for social inclusion as any of the other major events of the civil rights movement. Had it not been for her actions that day it is unlikely that the gradual progression towards acceptance of integration and inclusion for all people would have ever started to take hold on our thinking. It is also undeniable that there is still a long way to go.

Chapter 5 | The Recovery Story

'I'm going to become Dr Deegan and change the mental health system so that no one ever gets hurt in it again'

(Dr Pat Deegan)

Dr. Pat Deegan is one of the world's foremost advocates for people with mental health disorders. A hospital survivor, she recalls how diagnosis and sectioning almost ended her chance of having any active useful life.

Diagnosed at seventeen with 'schizophrenia with paranoid features' Dr. Deegan describes the devastating effects of the clinical judgement and its implications for her life.

In her lecture Recovery from Mental Disorders she states:

the fact that I was Pat, that there were many elements to my person became absolutely irrelevant…

My humanity became irrelevant. The fact that I

had friends, the fact that I was a good athlete, was irrelevant…

She goes on to explain that from the psychiatric point-of-view the prognosis on her was that:

this is a disorder not a person

Under the interventions of a hospital psychiatrist Pat Deegan was told that any future she had lay in the halfway house, social security and what she ironically refers to as 'a career in mental health'.

'A life of handicaptivity'

Pat Deegan was under a care team that felt her treatment was successful in that it stopped the progression of her illness.

But for her it was far from anything that resembled 'living' or getting remotely close to the kind of life she wanted. She describes it as being condemned to 'a life of handicaptivity'.

It was during this period that Deegan formulated the resolution that would change the entire course of her life and career. As she puts it: 'it was then I had a thought...one I had never had before':

'I'm going to become Dr Deegan and change the mental health system so that no one ever gets hurt in it again...'

Sparked off by that simple thought and braving years of struggle and determination, Pat Deegan has become one of the world's foremost champions of mental health recovery.

Ironically, Dr. Deegan never dared disclose that aspirational thought to any members of her care team at the time. She knew she would be labelled as 'delusional' and would no doubt be given increases in the medication that was already numbing her. Nonetheless the dream never left, becoming stronger as time went on.

The thought that Dr. Deegan dared not disclose to her psychiatrist was a 'eureka' moment. It is exactly the kind of aspirational announcement that any life coach would be overjoyed to hear from the mouth of a client. What life coach would not wish to hear something as clear and definite from his or her client like 'I want to become a doctor and change the face of healthcare'? What a magnificent life goal!

Without pioneers like Pat Deegan it is unlikely that life coaching and social inclusion techniques would ever have become available for people with diagnoses of severe and enduring mental ill-health.

Inclusion life coaching enables a language that permits clients and patients to address their goals, hopes and dreams. Under the restrictions of a purely diagnosis-led approach this was never the case previously.

Chapter 6 | How Shift Happened in the UK

Forerunners like Rosa Parks and Pat Deegan have helped enable a revolution in social inclusion and mental health.

In the United Kingdom, it took till the late 1990s and early 2000s before social inclusion as a strategy for mental health entered public discourse. Although some initiatives for independent living had been developed for people with long-term conditions, most of them revolved around support and management rather than recovery or returning to mainstream life.

Techniques were developed or adapted to enable clients with long-term mental health conditions to discuss their goals, hopes and aspirations in mainstream life. These were strategies commonly available to any professional life coach.

But this was the first time that these strategies had been incorporated into public health policy.

Mental health commissioners first had to be convinced that building a bridge between the client and the mainstream world would constitute an effective tactic. It would need to be cost-effective for one thing and ultimately it could serve to replace or work alongside, some of the existing network of other support services.

Also, a mainstream recovery service required outcomes that are measurable. What criteria were needed to show that clients had successfully made inroads into mainstream life? How much or how little support would each individual client need? What assessment tools were required? How much does it cost to recruit and train a team of bridge builders to enable clients to make their own independent choices in mainstream life?

Chapter 7 | The Tools of Social Inclusion Life Coaching

These slow but determined changes in social thinking led almost inevitably to a revolutionary turn of the wheel in public policies. The embracing of life coaching techniques for mental wellbeing became inevitable. In order for a revolution to take place it is not required for us to reinvent the wheel.

A Wheel of Life for Social Inclusion

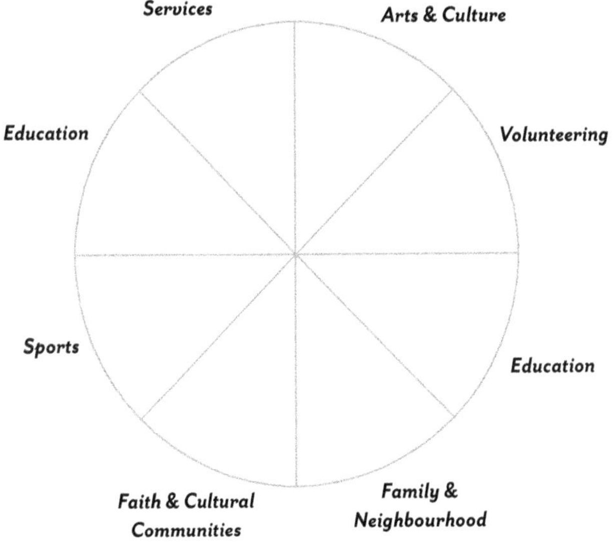

Life coaches are very familiar with the 'wheel of life' tool. It is this basic tool that was adapted for mental health and social inclusion commissioning in the early 2000s.

In the UK, the Inclusion Web concept was developed by Peter Bates and the National Development Team (NDTi) in the mid 2000s.

Substantial development and pilot work was carried out by Andrew Gibb and the team at the Mainstream project at Imagine, Liverpool.

It was the Imagine organisation that successfully brought social inclusion for mental health recovery into the heart of statutory mental health provision in the UK. Imagine won contracts for inclusion-based services in Liverpool and the northeast of England. The company went on to secure inclusion-based contracts in London and Surrey.

The championing of the idea that social inclusion should be the ultimate goal of a recovery-orientated health service was

driven not only by new ideas but also by practical financial reasons.

Shepherd, Boardman and Slade's 'New Horizons' research in 2008 showed that billions of pounds were being lost every year due to employee sickness, a substantial amount of it due to mental ill-health. National productivity was also taking a big hit as a result. Finally, the cost of providing support services to mental health survivors was often cost-ineffective and served to exclude people from returning to work or starting employment.

'Presenteeism' was also cited as a root cause of low productivity. Presenteeism is the phenomenon of employees turning up for work with undisclosed ill-health conditions or just undisclosed unhappiness.

The mantra hasn't really changed. The Prevention Concordat for Better Mental Health was launched by Public Health England in August 2017. The same issues and themes are highlighted: the haemorrhaging of public and private money through mental ill-health-related problems and the need for all sectors to collaborate in ill-health prevention. There can be little doubt that right now is the time for life coaching.

Back in the mid-2000s the organisation Imagine's successes with clients from backgrounds of long-term mental health diagnoses helped to convince commissioners that these 'mainstream' techniques were viable and affordable strategies for mental health recovery. Social inclusion coaching emphasises the point made by the New Horizons research that *'recovery takes place regardless of symptoms or problems'*.

This is crucial because it accepts that the management of a mental health condition might be a lifetime's work. For many people, it frequently is. Nonetheless, people with those conditions can still address their goals and aspirations and bring them to life in the mainstream world.

Social inclusion life coaching and the philosophy behind it means that we are equipped to start moving in a new direction away from purely support-based mental health service provision.
Let's turn now to have a detailed handbook eye's look at how the social inclusion web or wheel of life works.

The social inclusion 'web' coaching tool follows herein. An explanation of how it works for client, coach and commissioner is included and explained.

Chapter 8 | The Handbook of Social Inclusion Coaching

This section of 'Let Me do it Too!' is designed to show how social inclusion coaching tools work in practice. The examples I quote draw from material from coaching sessions with clients referred through statutory health services.

Evidence-based Research

There is a review of the 'web' coaching tool in 'Supporting Recovery in Mental Health Services: Quality and Outcomes' *(Shepherd, Boardman, Rinaldi and Roberts)* published by Centre for Mental Health in 2014:

- *The 'Social Inclusion Web' provides a practical resource to help individuals (or groups) chart and then monitor their progress regarding increasing community inclusion.*

- *It covers eight domains of social contact – employment, education, volunteering, arts & culture, faith and meaning, family and neighbourhood, physical activity and services – and assesses the number of people in the person's social network and the number of places that matter to them.*

- *The information is intended to be produced by a joint discussion between the person and their key worker and the results are presented in an easy-to-understand, 'clock' diagram. Data from 150 service users in Liverpool demonstrated good sensitivity to change and good content validity.*

Evidence-based research on the efficacy of the social inclusion web was crucial to its techniques being taken seriously by health commissioners in the early 2000s. This combined with a climate of social inclusion and the broad-based human rights movement helped to launch inclusion programmes in the mental health sphere. Government think tanks of the time took all the research onboard and this undoubtedly helped the rollout of inclusion programmes locally and regionally.

Fig 1 | THE SOCIAL INCLUSION 'WEB'

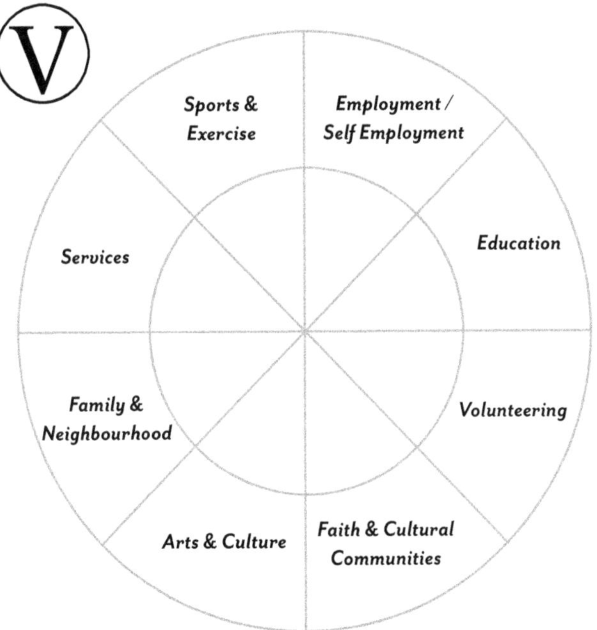

Fig 2 | *MEASUREMENT OF SOCIAL DOMAINS ACCESSED BY CLIENT*

(Information drawn from Client's Wheel of Life)

Mainstream Domain	*Places*	*People*
Employment		
Volunteering		
Faith & Cultural Communities		
Sport / Exercise		
Arts / Culture		
Services		
Family / Neighbourhood		
Education		
TOTAL		

Figs 1 and *2* pictured above are respectively the social inclusion web or wheel of life and *Fig 2* the assessment table. The web tool is designed to enable clients to identify areas of mainstream life in which they want to participate. These may be entirely new areas or ones that clients may have experienced previously, through their employment or social interests. Alternatively, it can be used to help clients identify areas they may have never had the chance to access before and wish to do now.

The coach's job is to listen non-judgementally to the client and guide him or her to building up a picture of their past, present and wished-for future. It provides a map that helps the client choose areas where he or she wishes to see change, growth and development.

The social inclusion wheel is not designed to prescribe specific social domains on behalf of the client. Nor is it designed to be a wheel that is completed in all sections, unless the client wants it to be. For example, a client may have no interest in doing sport or exercise. In that case, the section with that social domain does not need to be filled in. However, a client might mention that he or she has done some sport or exercise in the past and this can be noted on the wheel.

The assessment table *(Fig 2)* enables commissioners, clients and coaches to measure the client's progress in achieving outcomes in mainstream life. If commissioners have decided that access to mainstream living is important for mental health recovery, it follows that some way to measure clients' progress has to be devised. The assessment table in *Fig 2* is specifically designed for this purpose. *Figs 3* and *4* follow, showing results of a client/coaching first wheel of life session and a completed assessment table.

Life coaches know that the wheel of life tool can be adapted for individual clients. A client is free to use a blank wheel and fill in the segments independently, according to which areas he or she might wish to see change and development. The social inclusion wheel is relatively prescriptive in that it outlines the social domains that clients may not have had the opportunity to access previously.

The social inclusion wheel or 'web' has been designed to enable people who may not have the chance to join mainstream living or who have been excluded from it for months or years. It has been created for people with long-term mental health conditions to access the same arenas of life that many of us take for granted.

The social domains that appear on the inclusion wheel of life are grounded in the research that was carried out into areas of living that people identify as important or relevant. They are also the same domains that health commissioners consider to be a key part of an individual's mental health recovery. Crucially, these are the areas that commissioners have been willing to channel public money into, based on evidence-based research, positive outcomes and cost-effectiveness. It's worth reiterating the evidence-based research done by the Centre for Mental Health in 2014.

'The 'Social Inclusion Web' provides a practical resource to help individuals (or groups) chart and then monitor their progress regarding increasing community inclusion. It covers eight domains of social contact - employment, education, volunteering, arts & culture, faith and meaning, family and neighbourhood, physical activity and services - and assesses the number of people in the person's social network and the number of places that matter to them.'

(Supporting Recovery in Mental Health Services: Quality and Outcomes published 2014 by Centre for Mental Health)

'Supporting Recovery' clearly outlines the

eight domains of social contact, covering employment, education, volunteering, arts & culture, faith and meaning, family and neighbourhood, physical activity and services.

In practice, the client is not required to disclose information in every domain on the social inclusion wheel. Areas such as 'faith and meaning' might be irrelevant to some clients as much as they are highly significant for others. You will see from the inclusion web in *Figs 1* and *3* that 'Faith and Meaning' has been adjusted to 'Faith and Cultural Communities'. In practice this was more appropriate in order to distinguish between faith-based areas such as regular worship and other areas such as studying tai chi or learning meditation.

'Cultural communities' covers a wide area from things like learning cookery from world cultures or attending a specific venue or centre directly related to the client's own cultural background.

Not all domains will be as significant to some clients as they might be to others. For example, I have clients who have prioritised sports activity over the arts or clients who prioritise learning meditation over volunteering.

The important thing is that through the coaching consultation, clients can specify areas they wish to develop in mainstream life. The coach can help them to access these domains in a practical time-lined way. It is not the coach's job to apply his or her own values to clients' chosen pathways.

The third crucial section of the life coaching tools is the Action Plan *(Fig 3)*. The action plan is essentially a summation of the goals prioritised by the client during his or her coaching session. The action plan also serves to seal the contract between coach and client. The coach is contracted to help enable the client to achieve his or her prioritised goals in a practical and time-lined way.

Fig 3 | ACTION PLAN

(V)

Name of Coach: ....

Date: ....

Name of Client: ....

Areas Client Prioritises: (e.g.)

1) *Start weekly gym session*
2) *Do voluntary work one day a week*
3) *Meet up with my son*

Timescales

Client wishes to achieve these priorities in following period (e.g.)

1) *within one week*
2) *already commenced (charity shop volunteer)*
3) *by beginning of March this year*

Contract: I the coach am contracted to help enable the client achieve these prioritised goals in the timescales specified above by the client.

I the client pledge to work on my prioritised areas within the timescales I have specified above.

....

Signed (Coach) Signed (Client)

The Importance of the Action Plan

Action plans are commonly used in coaching consultations. For social inclusion life coaching, the action plan is particularly crucial.

The action plan is the place where the coaching contract is signed and sealed. In the action plan *(see Fig 3)* the coach signs the contract pledging to help the client achieve his or her stated priorities. In addition, the coach pledges under contract to work with the client to achieve these mainstream goals within stated timescales. The client signs to acknowledge that these are the areas he or she wishes to prioritise. The client also agrees to the timescales decided on the action plan. The client is equally contracted to achieving his or her goals as the coach is to seeing them happen for the client in the mainstream world.

For example in *Fig 3* the client has assigned a number one priority to attend gym on a weekly basis. The coach in turn has signed up to helping the client achieve this goal within one week of the signed date of the action plan contract. This is where social inclusion coaching starts generating profound value to its clients. The value arises from the decision to take action along with the first step of the action itself - the first visit to the gym.

People often ask me: 'isn't social inclusion coaching very time-intensive? Not only do you have to carry out coaching sessions with your clients but you also have to be a mentor to them don't you?'

I usually reply 'yes and no' to this question. Anyone who wishes to be an effective social inclusion coach needs to understand that a degree of mentorship is required. There's no doubt about that. Take the example of the client in *Figs 3* and *4*. He has stated and written up a desire to re-attend the gym and has made this a number one priority on his action plan. It might be that he requires the accompaniment of someone as an introduction back to the gym on the first occasion. This could be a friend, a carer or his life coach.

Social inclusion life coaches should never assume anything. Coaches should not take for granted that just because a client is from a background of mental ill health that he or she automatically requires support.

This is where the all-important necessity of inquiry comes into play. Coaches are often taught for the need to ask clients 'powerful questions'. But in social inclusion coaching there is often an even greater need for asking simple questions. Simple is powerful.

In this scenario, where a client has flagged up returning to regular gym work as a priority, the coach needs to ascertain how much or how little support the client requires to achieve this. So an appropriate question might be:

'Do you need someone to accompany you on the first visit back to the gym?'

The client will either answer 'yes' or 'no' to this question. He might tell the coach that a friend, carer or family member will go with him. He might want to go unaccompanied (which is often the case when people start back on the journey into mainstream living). He might request that the coach accompanies him on the first occasion.

If a client requires the coach to accompany him or her on the first visit to a mainstream venue, then the coach must be willing to do so. It is part and parcel of social inclusion life coaching. In my experience over a wide spectrum of mainstream venues, I have been asked to accompany clients on the first visit on around 50% of occasions. This is not a high percentage. When people start accessing or re-accessing mainstream life they are invariably keen to do so independently.

There are further questions that should be asked at the 'action plan' stage of the coaching consultation.

For example, the coach needs to ascertain whether the client intends to pay for the mainstream activity from his or her own funds. This is important for clients referred through health services because they may be on benefits of some kind. But it is equally important not to assume that a client from this group will be unable to afford to pay for his or her chosen activity. People with mental health conditions are the same as everyone else. They come in all shapes and sizes and from all kinds of financial backgrounds.

In my experience, the majority of clients I have worked with have been happy to pay for their mainstream activity themselves. Where this is not the case, the social inclusion coach should know how to access funding. It could be from a local personal budgets programme or from funds within your own organisation or the organisation that is hiring you. Sometimes life coaches have to become fundraisers too. I've done it myself and with great success.

So the question of whether social inclusion is time-intensive requires a flexible answer. In many ways social inclusion coaching is a lot less time-intensive than other kinds of life coaching. I have had many clients who have identified a mainstream goal and gone after it independently of the coach.

Case Study No. 3 | Linda's Story

Linda

Linda was referred to me from on of the other teams in our cluster. She had already had a coaching consultation and had identified music production as her one goal and priority. Since no one in our sister team knew of any recording studios in its catchment area, I was asked to step in. As a social inclusion coach specialising in the arts, it was part of my job to know where the arts and music venues operated in the mainstream community.

My coaching consultation with Linda stands as one of the most satisfying and successful of my coaching career.

I simply accompanied Linda to meet John, the manager at the recording studio. I left the two of them together to discuss whatever project it was Linda had in mind. I didn't hear from Linda for another six months. I knew she was attending the studio regularly and as a social inclusion coach, this is a positive mainstream result. Six months later I received a formal invitation by post to the public launch of Linda's new album of original compositions. This was an important moment for my client and represented the fruition of a lifelong dream. The launch was highly successful and led to Linda having compositions commissioned, doing radio interviews and starting on a career as a musician, composer and teacher.

The entire coaching consultation process with Linda comprised one meeting that contained both coaching and mentoring. If that's time and labour-intensive, then I welcome more of the same!

Chapter 9 | Social Inclusion Life Coaching for Groups

As life coaches know, coaching is not only appropriate for individuals but also for groups. Life coaching is being continually commissioned by organisations, company departments, by managers and in-house teams. There are some outstanding examples of in-house workplace coaching and development.

Swedish company IKEA has developed a 'Skills Escalator', which was introduced in 2002. The Skills Escalator comprises four steps where the employee begins as a trainee before stepping into their intended role. At the third step the person becomes a senior with the task of influencing and coaching others in their specialist role. The final step is master, which means that the employee has become an expert and mentor.

The same principle applies to social inclusion coaching for mental health and wellbeing. It is desirable to enable individuals to access or re-access mainstream living. But it is equally desirable to engage groups of clients for the same purpose.

Chapter 10 | How to Invite

When working with people referred from backgrounds of mental ill health we sometimes need to send out invitations. Individuals will not always choose social inclusion life coaching of their own volition. Sometimes this is because the mental health team omits to mention it as an option, sometimes because it isn't fully understood or because it gets overlooked. It can be the case that people under clinical teams perceive social inclusion mainstreaming as another clinical intervention. Clinical treatments such as therapies and counselling can be highly effective but life coaching provides a different strategy.

'Mister Fox's Night Out'

For this project I sent out invitations to

people with mental ill-health conditions to see if they wished to sign up for a series of animation and music production workshops. It was my first independent fundraising and social inclusion project. I worked in collaboration with ACAVA (Association for Cultural Advancement of the Visual Arts) as well as with the London borough of Merton arts development team.

The aims of the project were to enable people with long-term mental health conditions to access a mainstream arts project, using mainstream venues in the local community.

The remit was to enable a small team to learn animation techniques and music production. The outcome was to be a short animation film on a theme chosen by the group itself. The animation short was then to be shown at an international film festival. We achieved all of these outcomes.

With 'Mister Fox's Night Out' it was important for the team to choose its own subject matter and theme for the film. It was intended as a mainstream creative project, pure and simple. People with mental health conditions are occasionally commissioned to undertake creative projects of this kind but usually they are required to fit in with strict funding criteria. For example, films have been commissioned on prescribed themes. Some of the themes I have encountered have ranged from subjects like 'Depression' or 'Hate Crime'. These have been the kind of themes that are prescribed to clients by funders. They do not allow for the group or individuals to generate their own creative ideas from the outset.

There is nothing intrinsically wrong with this but in my opinion it limits the creativity of the team. Since I was the fundraiser for 'Mister Fox's Night Out' I was able to allow the team free rein to produce any kind of short animation film they wished within budget. I wanted to see an unencumbered mainstream outcome created by people who might not otherwise have the opportunity.

One participant summed up the experience like this: *'we started with nothing, got totally engaged, achieved a great deal and with an end product'*.

What do Health Commissioners Want to see Happen?

A project like 'Mister Fox's Night Out' was highly successful in terms of mainstream access, engagement and outreach for people with long-term mental health diagnoses. It was a freelance project that nonetheless fulfilled the criteria of any mental health commissioning team that works towards mainstream outcomes. Analysing the project from a commissioning perspective, it looks like this:

Mainstream Domain	***Places***	***People***
Employment		
Volunteering		
Faith & Cultural Communities		
Sport / Exercise		
Arts / Culture	3	14
Services		
Family / Neighbourhood		
Education	3	14
TOTAL	***6***	***28***

The breakdown of mainstream activity for just one participant in the film project 'Mister Fox's Night Out' shows that he / she has accessed mainstream venues and worked alongside fourteen people over a period of ten weeks.

For clients who also attended the film screening, a further mainstream 'place' can be added along with around 300 'people' who were also present at the venue.

From a commissioner's viewpoint, these are first-rate mainstream outcomes for the client's mental health care and recovery pathway.

There were six participants in total.

Fig 4 | *EXAMPLE OF A SOCIAL INCLUSION WHEEL OF LIFE WITH INFORMATION FROM FIRST COACHING MEETING WITH CLIENT*

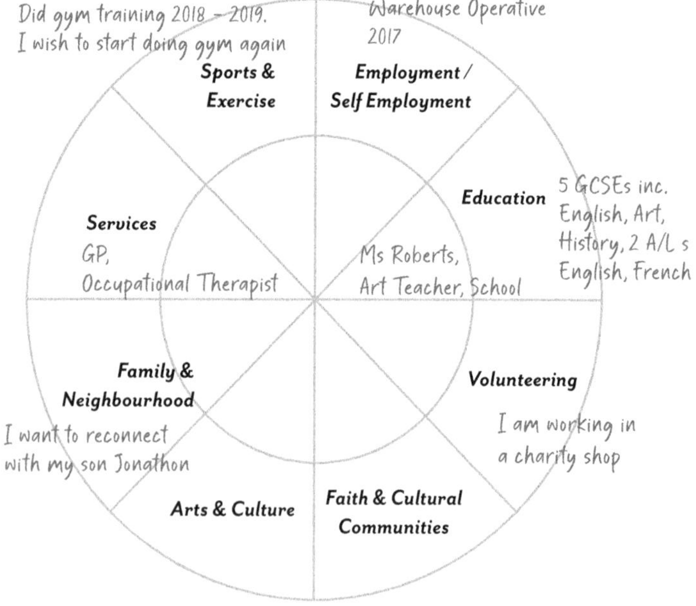

The Social Inclusion wheel of life contains eight segments denoting mainstream social domains. During the coaching session the client discusses in which domains he / she has been active and which domains he /she wishes to access further.

The outside of the wheel is used for the coach to note areas in the relevant domain which the client has previously accessed and also to note client's aspirations if he or she has any for that particular domain. In this wheel the client has expressed a wish to re-connect with his son. The coach has noted this goal on the outside of the 'Family / neighbourhood' segment of the wheel.The larger inner segment is used to note activities the client is currently doing. The third inner segments are used to note down significant people (past or present) in the client's mainstream activities.

Fig 5 | EXAMPLE OF A SOCIAL DOMAINS ASSESSMENT TABLE FILLED IN AFTER COACHING SESSION 1 WITH CLIENT

Mainstream Domain	*Places*	*People*
Employment		
Volunteering	1	15
Faith & Cultural Communities		
Sport / Exercise		
Arts / Culture		
Services	2	2
Family / Neighbourhood		1
Education		
TOTAL	*3*	*18*

THE SOCIAL DOMAINS

The Wheel of Life designed for social inclusion coaching is contains individual segments for specific social domains. As you can see from *Figs 1* and *3* there are eight domains in total. These are social domains of mainstream life that to one degree or another can be or have been relevant to individuals' lives. If a client has no interest in a specific domain then it can be left blank. If the client notes that the domain was once relevant to him or her in the past, that too can be noted outside the first rim of the wheel.

The social domains are also important for mental health commissioners. Those who commission mental health services are placing value in the ability of main-stream social inclusion for clients' recoveries. There has to be a way to measure and assess progress in mainstream life to ascertain its effectiveness, both in terms of cost and clients' continuing health. The assessment tables that appear in *Figs 2* and *5* form an integral part of the coaching and commissioning methodologies.

For example, the wheel of life in *Fig 3* is taken from the first coach/client consultation. It shows that the client was a warehouse operative from 2017, duly noted on the outside of the social domain segment for Employment / Self-employment.

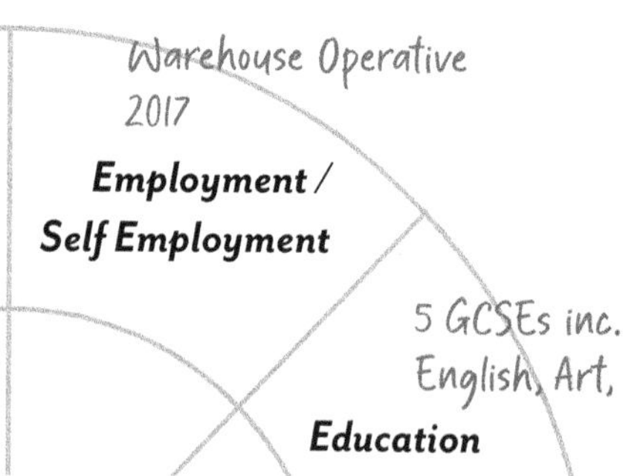

Similarly, the client (or coach transcribing from the client) has noted some educational qualifications on the outside of the 'Education' segment.

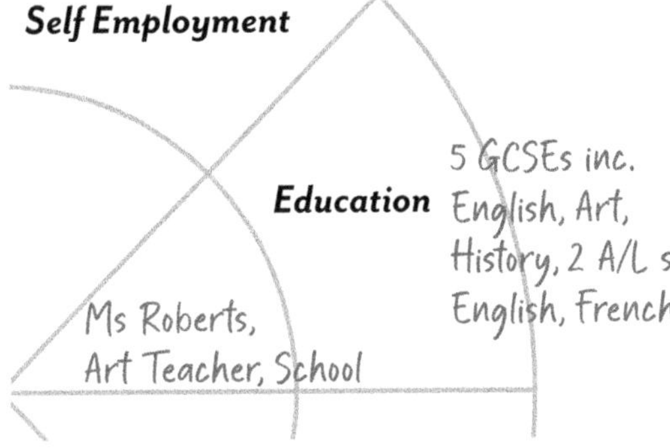

In the inner circle of the 'Education' social domain is the name of 'Ms. Roberts, Arts Teacher, School'. This is important because the coach is asking social inclusion clients to note any significant individuals in their past or present. It isn't essential that these individuals are active in the client's current activity. It simply helps to build up a picture, a 'map' of the client's mainstream life. It is also an important part of the coaching consultation. For some clients referred from backgrounds of mental ill health it can be heartening to recall that they once had active enriching mainstream lives. But these are important reminders for any of us.

In the segment that follows below, the client indicates that he did gym training in the past. He also notes the goal of taking up gym again.

Both previous activity and present goal are noted on the outside of the 'Sport / Exercise' social domain. Similarly, the client's goal of re-connecting with his son is noted on the outside of the 'Family / neighbourhood' segment.

A Tool that Measures Aspiration

The social domains that appear on an inclusion wheel are there to aid clients to re-access mainstream life based on their own choices, hopes and goals. These may be clients who have been 'out of the loop' due to mental ill health. They might be clients who have previously had glittering careers interrupted by episodes of illness. Mental ill health can happen to anyone.

The inclusion wheel is a coaching tool designed to introduce or re introduce these clients to mainstream activities of their own choice.

Above all, it is a tool that initiates a dialogue between the client and the mainstream world. It doesn't discriminate against people simply because they may have had episodes of ill-health or hospitalisation.

The coaching consultation allows individuals to identify areas where they wish to see change and generate a practical action plan to implement it. The social inclusion wheel of life has the same intention and drivers as any coach/client-generated wheel. For that reason it can be successfully utilised both for people referred from mental health services as well as for anyone else other. The only difference is that a client with a background of mental ill health may not have the same familiarity and experience of life in the mainstream community as some other clients might do.

In life coaching, the wheel of life can be built to serve the requirements of individual clients. In life coaching for social inclusion, the mainstream domains on the wheel are somewhat more rigorous. This is because as coaches we are attempting to help link individuals with mainstream living as part of their care and recovery pathways. The vision behind social inclusion coaching is that the mainstream world is itself a key part of the client's mental health recovery.

The social domains that appear on the wheels of life in Figs 1 and 3 are not written in stone. It may well be that clients wish to identify other mainstream areas that are as important to them. In those cases, the social inclusion web can be modified if required.

I have used the social inclusion wheel of life as it appears here in *Figs 1* and *3* on scores of occasions with my clients. In every case it has never failed to filter out the areas that clients identify as important to their growth as individuals wishing to engage or re-engage with mainstream life.

The Action Plan

Once those domains (it may be just one domain) have been identified by the client it is the coach's duty to draw up a SMART time-lined action plan with the client *(see Fig 5)*. Armed with the action plan, the coach can proceed to link clients up with mainstream venues where they can start or re-commence mainstream activity.

Mainstream Outcomes

Using these tools and strategies with an average of four to five sessions with my clients I have been able to link people up with a wide variety of activities, all of which take place outside clinical or day care settings. My specialisation lies in the arts and music in particular. As a result, clients have been able to do a wide range of activities based on their own choices, hopes and goals. These range from returning to college, accessing recording studios to rehearse and record music, learning jewellery design, studying creative writing and publishing, re-engaging with painting and exhibiting work in public venues, learning film and producing 'shorts' shown at international festivals.

Clients may well identify areas outside of the arts or outside my own specific specialisations. For example, the client's wheel of life in *Fig 3* shows that the client has expressed a wish to re-connect with his adult son. This is a mainstream aspiration and must be honoured under the coaching contract.

Similarly, a client might aspire to do sports or volunteering. He/ she might want to get back into employment or self-employment. A client might want to go back to church or temple or learn tai chi and meditation. As can be seen in the wheel of life in *Fig 3*, the client expresses a desire to re-establish the relationship with his adult son.

Clarity

One of the great strengths of the life coaching consultation is that a client can often start on the road to making changes simply by identifying the change in the first place. Writing it up on the wheel of life reinforces the client's intention. The action plan that follows is generated together by coach and client. This helps to cement clarity, intention and practical action.

Conscientiously followed, all the steps in the mainstream consultation will lead inevitably to practical outcomes for the client.

Conclusion

'Let Me Do That Too!' is designed to show that social inclusion life coaching techniques can be of immense positive value. The positive impact of these techniques continues to generate powerful outcomes for those who choose to seek out its coaching methodologies.

I have outlined some of those positive outcomes in this book, along with a step-by-step guide for anyone interested in using these techniques in their own coaching practice.

Health commissioners too will derive benefit from 'Let Me Do That Too!' The book reveals assessment tools that have already been used by commissioners to measure clients' progress and establish cost-effective parameters for ongoing health budgets.

The case studies and tools that appear in the book are used in my own coaching practice. They are also tried and tested by evidence-based research, particularly that done by Centre for Mental Health.

It will be clear from anyone reading this book that the author's practice is derived substantially from my work with individuals and groups who have been referred from backgrounds of long-term mental ill-health.

My motivation for working with this group is not because I have any great clinical knowledge of mental illness. I do not claim to have such knowledge. However, I am passionate that people with long-term conditions should never be excluded from the benefits of life coaching.

Too often people with these conditions have been constricted by the limitations of a clinical diagnosis. Diagnoses are useful. They enable people to access support, medication and welfare when it is needed. However, I believe no one should be defined by his or her clinical diagnosis. Everyone should be allowed to address his or her goals, hopes, dreams and aspirations. Life coaching permits this to happen. Life coaching creates a level playing field where human beings can grow.

www.ingramcontent.com/pod-product-compliance
Ingram Content Group UK Ltd.
Pitfield, Milton Keynes, MK11 3LW, UK
UKHW020226250726
13967UKWH00001B/211

9 781999 637019